See the Sun and Be Yourself

See the Sun and Be Yourself

RICHARD A. RAMPELLO

RESOURCE *Publications* • Eugene, Oregon

SEE THE SUN AND BE YOURSELF

Copyright © 2021 Richard A. Rampello. All rights reserved. Except for brief quotations in critical publications or reviews, no part of this book may be reproduced in any manner without prior written permission from the publisher. Write: Permissions, Wipf and Stock Publishers, 199 W. 8th Ave., Suite 3, Eugene, OR 97401.

Resource Publications
An Imprint of Wipf and Stock Publishers
199 W. 8th Ave., Suite 3
Eugene, OR 97401

www.wipfandstock.com

PAPERBACK ISBN: 978-1-6667-3280-1
HARDCOVER ISBN: 978-1-6667-2689-3
EBOOK ISBN: 978-1-6667-2690-9

.   OCTOBER 19, 2021 11:58 AM

Contents

PART I *WHERE I AM POEMS*

The Welcome | 3

And So It Starts | 4

Purpose of the Propose | 5

Driven by More than Purpose | 6

Looking Where? | 7

Emergence Can Seek | 8

It Was an Effort | 9

Cornier than Candy | 10

Simplicity Has No Bounds | 12

Oh, the Depths | 13

I See You | 14

Transition to the Land of Shakespeare | 15

PART II *SERIES OF CONVERSATIONS: PLAY FORMAT*

Act I, Scene I | 19

Act I, Scene II | 25

Act II, Scene I | 30

Act II, Scene II | 31

Act III, Scene I | 32

In Conclusion | 33

PART III *SERIES OF TALKS*

Cliché Comes from Somewhere | 37

The Flow | 39

Eye | 41

Talking to Myself | 43

Waiting on the Listen | 44

The Moment | 45

To Bid Adieu | 46

Part I

Where I Am Poems

This is how I got to where I am

THE WELCOME

Life anew from you
From the unseen is glue
Heat intensified to blue
A reminder to say thank you
From a world of the subdued
Once a soul always cued
Rigid as it blows through
Because from the unseen came glue

AND SO IT STARTS

The ball of light rests in hand
My heart his guide
To rise is to cover our land
Removed from a slippery slide
From in to out
Eyes are a happy spout

PURPOSE OF THE PROPOSE

Don't rush or amble,
Yet we try to trust and gamble
At this game we call life
From love to strife
The best things from spouse or wife
Are from the game we call life

DRIVEN BY MORE THAN PURPOSE

Let me be more than me
More than him or he
From countenance to digits
Even a big guy fidgets
To you and all, let me be
For you are better than thee
Better than They or He
A gift to grow like a tree
Breathe in the generated rays
And let me be the one who stays

LOOKING WHERE?

With a head like a balloon
Or a lady befallen by swoon
A simple poke could be an issue
While away head, I miss you
Returned to a rightful lair
Something is missing up there
Could it be hair?
Perhaps now you need a tissue?
With that word
I feel absurd
To issue such softness from thy
Especially when you ask why

EMERGENCE CAN SEEK

In the trenches of wrenches and ache
Can be benches and very little opaque
For fury is focus when tempered just right
Before it becomes a locus of cannibalizing fright
A drive that is safe can still score
Whilst a path with no strafe could bore
For see unto your heart from mind
To mine the desire from blind
Note, oh good one, the fight of
Another son in light of
A forgotten one in pun alight
With the fury of focus when tempered just right

IT WAS AN EFFORT

It starts with how was it, how did I use my tool?
Sometimes it's a noodle but I'm no jelly-like fool
So I turn and say of my day of structure and thought
I will always feel I took more than I brought
But my teacher, my education purveyor
Makes me feel smart as I become a conveyor
Supported by the idea I can talk about what I was taught
Knowledge is a race to run where you're never caught
Different subjects, ideas, lines to ponder
Ones I will use and comprehend yonder
To amble with intention, yet still let my mind wander . . .

CORNIER THAN CANDY

As my day ends, so to it begins again
To my planner and curriculum go my pen
Instructors must always challenge without being pushy
Education is never lax nor should it be cushy
To be the best, you must work very hard
Forget not your dreams or running in the yard
That is later and I tell you because learning is fun
There is no such thing as too much or none
The brain can always allow and permit
So please focus up front, here, as you sit
Fret not of embarrassment to try to answer
Be respectful to adults with ma'am or sir
I am getting you ready for the world somehow
Let us focus first on here and now
Because the days of structure start early
Remember to brush and floss the pearly
Before that to consume a healthy bite
After a restful night to avoid partly opened sight
The days of structure can seem so long
Yet in order to grow time must prolong
To halt distracters and improve focus
You see to garner knowledge is work, not hocus-pocus
The days of structure are a necessity
Myriad or many subjects to cover is key
The days of structure call for cleanliness
Emitting a good smell starts with a tress
Well, all of them, your hair and your face
Prepare the night before to avoid the morning race

On time for the bus or be ready to walk
To interact when appropriate as I talk
So why do I learn how to present and what to do?
A big part of your life is work and how you become you

SIMPLICITY HAS NO BOUNDS

To be president you must be thirty-five
And a citizen of America's hive
You could be a judge, a senator or in lower tiers
To perhaps not deal with the world's fears
Surely it can be more complicated
But your impact cannot be dated
Dream to be something more,
Because ambitions are not a chore
Perhaps you could grow and sow
Work as a farmer is not for public show
So maybe it is a dream to sing or act
But practical importance should remain intact
A balance between what you could or may be
A police officer, garbage person or an emcee

OH, THE DEPTHS

See the beam of light bestowed upon plight
Shake the fruits of labor without slight
Shown the back, but stifled by fear
You have created such a sight
A line, non-linear, albeit still so clear
The gift is clarity in the shadow
Of crisis, to show
What we already know
And yet the mold is not old
Fresh with a scent quite bold
Distilled by effort and acceptance
A secular, intimate penance

I SEE YOU

It is said success can be defined
Or perhaps updated and refined?
Fearing the unexpected
Is intermittently respected
Betrothed to success
While sans excess
Put life in jest
From the infusion of zest
A lemon, a lime, an orange
Citron, citron vert, l'orange
It's not an, but a tricky
Rhyme from an icky
Time to be sublime
Colored like slime
How many times?
A question of times
A world of mimes
Like millions in dimes
But oh the round is found
Downed like a pound
I see you defined
As we work on the refined
Out in front, atop and behind
The son who continues to find

TRANSITION TO THE LAND OF SHAKESPEARE

Onward to a journey begun
Using a homonym is fun
Ah, but which one?
From the darkness of done
Sparks the rise of this fun
No longer undone to ring
By mourning
Or morning
Oh, please see what fun
Was done

Part II

Series of Conversations: Play Format

These deal with where I have been and show the evolution — and revolution — of life

ACT I, SCENE I

At Thine House of Covered Ivory. The telly is being played out, only there is nothing visually seen. A gathering is evident as well. Camera clicks are heard.

P: Restoration as past tense acting merit can justify a crestfallen countenance, heretofore,
though, sturdiness is guaranteed in nothing.
E.T., be in country or being, being cited by a short-sighted aim inverted,
begs for additional scruples to be mined and examined Purification? The 20 discussed this burn,
they mete the destruction of thine only hallowed,
whilst what follows in a backed up fiber production
Figurative and perhaps intentionally literal
The ideal is figurative, options also, reactions the same,
yet I return to thine above reminder definition thereof they are not.

Cross Country at an unassuming, straightforward home. Mi and M. are finishing up a day. N. is upstage left focused on the computer.

Mi: Yo, Holmes by the creek, off to see Bert.

Pause.

Mi: Er, one should have given pause

M: Unto yourself sans this audible remorse. Retirement beckons.

Mi: Warm reception to the subconscious.
M: Aye.

Erstwhile in the house, T. enters as M. exits, both stage left. Their paths cross.

T: To improv and unfettered?

M: Or so desired. Adieu.

T: Adieu.

Mi: Aye, adieu.

(T. looks hastily paused.)

Mi (With a wry curve slowly ascending): Doth the unapproved, as to only be expected, in tow? A la Jack?

T: Spoken too accurately, A. exists no longer. You know?
Mi: Specks?

T (sarcastically but pained): Aye. Specks as in disconnected freckles. Ti's the handcuffs of opportunity.

Mi: The head is downed.

T: Wherefore? Ti's he? Cease it.

Mi: A. seemed transparent, meaning respect and entwined. Regret is expressed in discomfort, you know if.

T: I am unlike the rose, or rather like a particular one. I know it is gotten.

Mi (returned playfully as well): Merci. Perhaps his rose has scruples somewhere.

(T. looks to interrupt only to hold back. Mi is transfixed.)
Mi (Commenting on the telly): Saltine holds weight, or the references to George - irony as founded
by Brown -
is truly past. Is truly morphemes. Immediate reaction
to reach for saltine is a reflection of self-actualization through
the peepers of another. It is an attempt, an effort,
to be unified through coercion.

T (laughing with a head shake): Although unlike thriller, some prints are in step. (More serious tone now) Ti's twilight, but comprehended.

(N. turns to face Mi and T. downstage. His attention is now piqued.)

N: It is like the script just past. What is perceived is not guaranteed or fast.

Mi: No ill shalt slip.

N: Structure doth not remand or loose Him. The Him.
The Him-

Mi: Or Her, although definition does not imprint me. Pardon.

N (Mockingly defiant): The Him is the trump card that places all others. P. sees subservience as I do. Yum-yum.

T (slightly divisive): Relic.

Mi: Ti's halted, for relic was an inadvertent acquiesce.

N (passionately): Lose not what was never lost, even if never seemingly found.

Mi (after a pause and with clear contriteness; some derision, albeit unintentionally): Known. Appreciated. (Softening) Ti's difficult. A return is to be made. Onward.

N (slightly disappointed): All right. Furthermore, there is irony here like the Farrow critic.

Mi (proudly and impressed): Your eyes found it?

N: Aye.

Mi (permitting the moment). No nay here. Agreed.
(An air of calm and momentary resolution is evident for the moment).

Mi: I shalt follow the last exit
Requirements?

T: Nay. Adieu.

Mi (hugging T.): Adieu. Like the male who crows may one find the other one.

T: Aye. Thanks.

(To N.)

Mi: Ditto.

N (maturely): Ditto. Adieu.

Mi: Adieu.

T: Tread securely.

Mi: Not taken lightly.

(Mi exits stage right).

(Meanwhile, P is settling down with F.)

F: Beaten not by the beating.
One, yourself, is so enabled as
hubris stands in the course.

Great swat

P: Myriad reflections of praise unto thine motivation,
albeit not singular.

F: (slyly, almost playfully): Fatigue and judgement will curtail any additional.
(Plain speech, not preachy) You spake of contempt forged through in duty.
I speak. Noted?

P (a smirk evident): Aye.

F: The eyes of the world are here now. Do not cross into sardonic, P.

P (with humor): Tally yet another.

F: In the sight of all, the lexicon of notability, the rooted 400 shalt never roam.
Ti's the steps of He, the steps of you,
I,
and the continuous let down. Well, I wish to bid adieu.
And bid adieu.

P (with sarcasm): The duplicitous broach with a direct intention; (With thought) the elevated a prorated with uniform, some di-

F: P.! The hands.

P (a worried look gives way to a smile): the gap gaped certainly.

F (yawning): I follow suit.

P: Adieu.

F: Again, and finally, Adieu.

P/F (They look at one another and remark in near synch): Adoration for thee.

(The curtain falls. The day has ended).

ACT I, SCENE II

The day awakens

Mi (Groggily before warming up to a sarcastic tone): Thy courier of sorts needs?
Singularly driven do I recall in loop
Truancy only in, well, I relent it was a sale, instead
Birthed in a lapse of official (a huff punctuates this line, indicating an anger is brooding)
Not his Maker but a caretaker, instead
Stead all right
Preternatural occurrence?
As is the second call hef
Noosed is all those that …
Pish-posh now
One is of contribution, or at least of hold

(Mi leaves as everyone is sleeping at the aforementioned mentioned house in Act I)

N (at his computer): Wherefore in a duplicitous bit,
for freed of deliberate, albeit unintentional, or
maybe …
There are no answers

B (interrupting N's thoughts; almost with a pain in her voice): Hmm
Slumber light?
N (almost emotionless): Ponder overtakes me

B (sympathetically): Doth to all.
To break?

N: Fret nothing

B (a soft confidence, with a direct effort at being verbose, although on a lesser scale): Aye
Like the golden circle
and the staunch of
belief; good or evil
Well, the lessening of all right, perhaps?

N (with a wry wit): Noted and humbled

B (same type of wit, although a bit troubled) Innovative not, eh?

N (staunchly): I reiterate as before sans indignant sense
Forgiveness, aye?

B (softly): Aye.

(Meanwhile, across the way, Mi hast arrived and walks into a room, where he is met by the co-worker).

NM (with relative earnest): And so it occurs. Time is now.
With salute.

Mi (straight-forward and with honest reflection): Aye.
I create the same mat.
Just a step or so.

NM (unmoved with nod): Comprehended.

(The day proceeds)

Mi (to K who has been in and out): Decision?

K (inadvertently derisive): Has the other warmed the core? Iced the blaze?

Mammon (waltzes sans rhythm in with an unforced huff): Mi, to thine layer off the course.

Mi (resolute from standard): Procession in effect.

(After some time K has supplanted Mi at station, where Mi proceeds to the layer)

Mammon (coldly): Who ye be is not the fee here
It be what you are,
Although what you are in present
could lend; however,
it is not of, certainly

(He presents a paper to Mi, who is stifling. Mammon continues unstaunched.)

Resolute is this, for reception is not gotten.

(Ka is seated to Mammon's left, looking unsympathetic).

(coldly still, even though an effort to warm is gruffly being pushed through) Release from countenance?

Mi (a bit meekly, eyes lowered): Nay.

Mammon (unmoved, almost relieved): The stamp comes forth.
Yours to be here (points to his desk).
Return I will

Ka (with an uncomfortable sympathy, well practiced): Thy rigid way can offer an ease
Do as effective's part
Thou's statement, for the one parted,
leaves thy option supple

Mi (upset but measured): His oversight is deterred
As well as outright misguided
Its absence has no partner in fondness

(Ka quietly appears to muse. Mammon enters shortly thereafter, with, seemingly, purpose.)

Mammon (resolutely and unflinching): Make as the leader of thing first congress

(Mi begrudged with an eye fierceness, aimlessly pointed away. There is more than disappointment unveiled. He looks almost betrayed as well as dismayed.)

Mammon (without breath in the moment): You shall be sidled.

(Mi almost a step behind follows, but not in lurk. The door is held opened and Mammon speaks emotionlessly):

The service is noted.

Mi (with a snap): Like a mass grave.

(Mi returns to the dwelling from which he rose that morning, an undeterred ride, clearly perturbed. He enters his dwelling, where G. enters from the hallway, entering on the left to the kitchen, meeting Mi as he enters the same room):

G. (with a pleased look): Thine day?

Mi (trying to hide the events of the day from his countenance, although he is unable to hide that he is perturbed): The day.

G. (inquisitively, with good intent): The call?
Err, your call?

Mi (flatly, in effort to not have more information pulled from him):
There is no call.
Superfluous intervened
The all in, apparently, is
the way out.
Yet the adage of perfection reams more truth,
a forgotten believability and wonton reality,
of what is not to be obtained.
Perhaps perception is back (a slight bemused smile crosses his lips as he finishes that line)?

ACT II, SCENE I

Mi: Before post-hoc is, well,
As etre points out, is
Descartes and existentialism
is presented in grounds;
idolized in ideals or the idyllic
Pull up like an Italian brethren

P (sighs) See reality is all I ask?

Mi: Huh?

P (hands data to Mi): This is I
Recall it

Mi (defiantly): Aye. Yet this is spoken
Your presentation surmises

P (resigned): Aye

ACT II, SCENE II

M (with reserve): It is as thought

Mi (Resigned, albeit forcibly tempered): It is. Aye?

M: I return

Mi: Planted I should-

M: Nay. Speak no further. Not one iota. Note the stated, and recall the strength

Mi (cringing): Aye. And you?

M (Looking slightly down, eyes lowered, lower lip trembling): You know . . .

Mi: Concurred.

ACT III

Mi: Wherefore the dip of know?
Seeing in wait,
While waiting to be viewed
Yet so pristine in sincerity
Unlike programming of politic,
And with great coverage the same,
Dost I . . . proceed?
Continue? Review? Reflect?
Existentialism in the standstill
And in the finite lies infinite
T'is not curiosity kept at bay,
Rather it is the ultimate fervor
Perhaps my countenance recedes?
Pride is not hurt
Oh, it's noted, but
Respect the power of knowing
It's okay to be unknown
Excuse nothing
See all while
Understanding nothing
To end is

IN CONCLUSION

We must seek in order to see rotund
Or the denial continues its run
From the dwelling of a lair unseen
Comes an unknown answer;
An answer actually known and clean
The round sung with a bit of coy
Is a reminder that from above comes joy
To mesh the worlds so divergent
Is to remind us of what is not urgent
Precious and timely, yes
Specious, occasionally in rhyme, yes
Note the touch, now renewed
With a slung yellow stone of sorts
Ah, the allure of derivative
Oh, the pieces are lost, but the
Puzzle rebirthed
A fealty unearthed
The hand is known with a path shown
But note no fate, but a symbolism of innate
That is why we can see the sun
And be yourself

Part III

Series of Talks

Life moves forward in learned fashion

CLICHÉ COMES FROM SOMEWHERE

Man, if you could see
Ever so bluntly
Your acknowledgement of pun
And the impact that was begun
Still how there is a reaction before pause
From the aftermath of cause
Maybe you would
Or maybe you wouldn't
You did what you could
Oftentimes what you should
And because of what you shouldn't
There is a fill of couldn't
Oh, but known is advice
A conversation to entice
What would it be?

And so there is discussion:

D: I see what remains
I assuredly see the gains

Mi: You'll seduce the notion of not begotten
But the glimpses only cover the rotten

D: But look at the unforgotten
The ill-conceived
See what you hast grasp
And cease with the gasp

Look at the unforgotten

Mi: Yes, a façade of what might be
To package so neatly
Oh, the hit is deeply
Noted, but a forge does not need to be so steeply
Gorged with what was
Or what is held intently

THE FLOW

I could hear the call –

MO: Staunch in integrity, now do the same

Mi: Aye, so imprinted

MO: See what is to be seen

Mi: Now the bend comes to turn
Comes the bulbous of what has risen

MO: See the what in what has arisen
Formalize what has arose

Mi: To gesture the reach

MO: It hast adorn the crest of two-fold

Mi: Betterment is presented
And away goes the flow of MO
Before the findings, so speaks the fire

SD: (Gurgle as the lever was lifted)

Mi: What was risen now slows and turns down
The newest comes from so little,
And begrudge it not
See the pity, perhaps compassion

Of the impassioned
To perhaps remind of why the lever was lifted
But an identifier finds thee
Perhaps a moment of visit from all three

EYE

The multiplicity of taking in
The duplicity of upward and downward eyes
Careful with act of sin
Or is it a freedom prize?
A cracker or a fit of impropriety
Humor is found amongst piety
See this continuity?
Observe that run?
Avoid the brown, although
Two find the bun
It's complicated, or maybe it's not
It's a twisted use of words like hot
And then there are the ones a spud doth sprout
A failure, but usability is still a factor

P: Did you spake?

Mi: Watch the snake, mind the grout and
It could cause lights out

P: Archived?

Mi: Dost one choose to defy and let fly

P: Pointed

Mi: Just be cautious with where
P: With sincerity?

Mi: Aye.

P: (Mildly bemused)

Hey, it's the kingdom we all must enter
And a catchy little ditty
And a fun spin on a spinning terror, projecting
A metaphor that is in reality a why
So we spot the dots of a blinking truck
Those two studious pupils that leave us saying aye.

TALKING TO MYSELF

It echoes, the beat and vocals
Seeing something bestowing focals
Oh, Mr. Silverstein
You impacted the adult and the teen
Not so much a Ra guy
But is that a presence of sky?
The life of ants
The dance of plants
To fulfill is a prance
Possibly substantial, if possible
Wants can stem from needs
But note distinction
Or face extinction
Even when shuttered
The rays find their way
It's not a silhouette as we get
Better yet
I have been buttered
Only to be muttered
But without rudder I am not
See the boat, note the moat
And remember the vastness of ocean
Roundabout the curve of the earth
As it circles the center
Mundane to so many others
So find the center

WAITING ON THE LISTEN

Mi: And so it wanes

Wi: And with wave I suppose?

Mi: Swing around to denote other

Wi: And so settles to the soul

Mi: One doth comprehend,
But the soul is muti-faceted
So is duplicity

Wi: Weigh the weight
What is known is known
See the mister of monastery

Mi: It lacks not
To be resolute is the push
The drive spoken of, and yet
To be precarious is the push
Connate conundrum

Wi: Do so also

Mi: Aye
Adoration for thee

Wi: Adoration for thee

THE MOMENT

The moment of ecstasy
Of recognition
To announce
To renounce
The moment of rejection
Realized
Feared
Of joy
The moment of incoherence
The sheer moment of reality
The moment lacking volume

Mi: Seen is the spread of gold
And seen was myself

The moment of disgust
Of rust
Of trust
Without bust
The moment of bustle
Of hustle
With no tussle
With no fuss
The moment of . . .

Mi: Regurgitation (the upper lip curl from the unfurl of hurl humor)
But intangible is more fun

TO BID ADIEU

Farewell
Good Bye
Good journey
Bid thee well

A wave
A finger
A peck
A zinger

Dramatic
Unfocused
Meandering
Pragmatic

Dogmatic
Secular
A prayer in flash
Automatic

Think not of the rise
Certainly breeds surprise
A role to be reprised
Power to supersize

Mi: A favor taken
Or a bow flaked in
Good intent

To be finite in the way
You see the sun
And be yourself

www.ingramcontent.com/pod-product-compliance
Lightning Source LLC
Chambersburg PA
CBHW061300040426
42444CB00010B/2444